Mapping Britain's Landscapes

Hills and Mountains

Jen Green

W

FRANKLIN WATTS
LONDON • SYDNEY

First published in 2007 by Franklin Watts

Copyright © Franklin Watts 2007

Franklin Watts
338 Euston Road
London NW1 3BH

Franklin Watts Australia
Level 17/207 Kent Street
Sydney, NSW 2000

Series editor: Sarah Peutrill
Art director: Jonathan Hair
Design: White Design
Consultant: Steve Watts
Picture research: Diana Morris
Additional map illustrations: John Alston

A CIP catalogue record for this book is
available from the British Library.

Dewey number: 526.09141
ISBN: 978 0 7496 7112 9

Printed in China

Franklin Watts is a division of
Hachette Children's Books, an
Hachette Livre UK company.

Picture credits:
Graham Bell/PD: 13.
Anthony Cooper/Ecoscene/Corbis: 19.
Ashley Cooper/Corbis: 25.
Chris Fairclough/PD: 15.
Mark Gwilliam/PD: 17.
Alain Le Garsmeur/Corbis: 21.
London Aerial Photo Library/Corbis: 7.
Brian Moyes/PD: 8.
Ordnance Survey © Crown copyright 2007 supplied
by mapsinternational.co.uk: front cover l, 4, 9, 10,
12, 14, 16, 18, 20, 23, 24, 27, 28, 29.
Dan Santillo/PD: 1, 11.
Skyscan/Corbis: 5.
Webb Aviation: 22.
Wild Country/Corbis: 26.

Every attempt has been made to clear copyright.
Should there be any inadvertent omission please
apply to the publisher for rectification.

Note to parents and teachers: Every effort has
been made by the Publishers to ensure that the
websites in this book are suitable for children, that
they are of the highest educational value, and that
they contain no inappropriate or offensive material.
However, because of the nature of the Internet, it is
impossible to guarantee that the contents of these
sites will not be altered. We strongly advise that
Internet access is supervised by a responsible adult.

Contents

What are hills and mountains?

Mountains and hills are areas of high ground that stand above the surrounding landscape. Many of Britain's mountains and hills are wild places with beautiful scenery. Learning to read maps can help you get to know them.

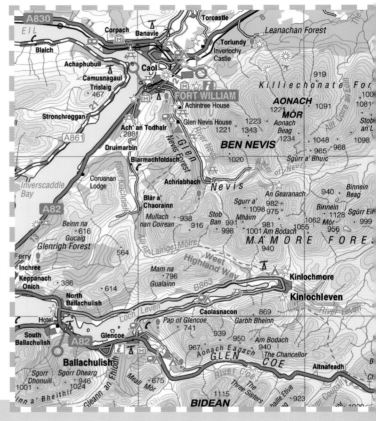

HILL OR MOUNTAIN?

In Britain, all peaks of high ground above 500 m are classed as mountains. Many mountains are craggy, with steep sides. Hills are lower and often more rounded. Many mountains are found in groups called ranges, such as the Grampian Mountains in Scotland. High peaks are separated by valleys or plains which form the lowlands.

↓ Using the map

What are maps?
Maps are drawings of the landscape from above, like the view from a plane. Maps show everything much smaller than in real life, so they have to leave out a lot of detail. To make things simpler, they only show permanent features – things that stay the same, such as mountains, roads and towns.

Cars, people and other details aren't shown. Maps use colours and also symbols (signs) to show mountains, towns, roads and other features. A key explains what the symbols mean. This atlas map shows the Grampian Mountains region in Scotland, which include Ben Nevis, Britain's highest mountain. Find these features:

 Land above 400m

Forest

 Land below 200 m

 Peak or high point

↑ **This is Britain's highest peak, Ben Nevis, with the town of Fort William below it.**

- Compare the photo and the map. What details can you see on the photo that aren't on the map?

- What information does the map give that you can't see in the photo?

- Why are the mountains in the photo snowy, when the lowlands have no snow?

MOUNTAIN WEATHER

Mountain temperatures are colder than the lowlands because mountain air is thinner (less dense) than air in the lowlands. Thin air holds less of the Sun's heat. In cold weather moisture falls as snow, which lingers on the mountain tops.

TAKING IT FURTHER

Ben Nevis is 1,343 m high. Fort William lies at sea level, so it's 1,343 m to the top! Find out the height of the nearest hill or mountain from your local map. Subtract the height where you live from this figure to work out the climb to the top.

How do hills and mountains form?

Hills and mountains are formed by upheaval deep below ground, which affects the rocks at the surface. Deep underground, the rocks are so hot they flow like a sticky liquid. The hard outer crust is made up of giant sections called tectonic plates.

FOLD MOUNTAINS

Red-hot rock flowing deep underground sets the surface plates drifting a few centimetres each year. As they drift, some of the giant slabs of rock crash together. The land between crumples upwards to form a type of mountain called a fold mountain.

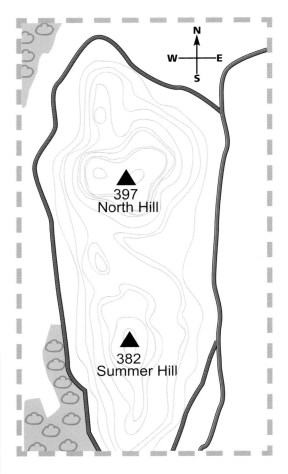

↓ Using the map

Contour lines
The map shows the Malvern Hills. The ups and downs of hills, mountains and valleys are shown on flat maps using lines called contour lines. Contour lines join places at the same height above sea level. On steep slopes, contour lines are shown close together. Figures called spot heights give the height of a particular place. Find these features:

 Contour line

 Spot height

VOLCANOES

Volcanoes sometimes erupt at the borders between plates. Red-hot melted rock surges upward to spill out at the surface. Long ago, Britain had active volcanoes.

Many hills and mountains in Britain are either fold mountains or made of volcanic rocks such as the Malvern Hills in Worcestershire.

← **This photograph shows the Malvern Hills from the air looking north.**

Look at the photo and the map

→ **Compare the photo and the map. What features shown on the map can't be seen in the photo?**

→ **Contour lines don't appear on the photo. What features help you to see the shapes of the hills?**

→ **Which would you find most useful on a hike in the Malverns, the photo or the map?**

TAKING IT FURTHER

• See for yourself how fold mountains form using a tablecloth. Spread your hands wide on the cloth and then press them closer together. The cloth scrunches upward into folds like a range of fold mountains.

• Find out more about tectonic plates, fold mountains and volcanoes by using the Internet or your local library.

• Find the Malvern Hills on a UK atlas. How does the height of these hills compare with mountain ranges on the map?

Cliffs and block mountains

Where two tectonic plates collide or scrape past one another, the rocks between are put under great pressure. Eventually the rocks shatter along deep cracks called faultlines. This can create dramatic features such as steep mountains and sheer cliffs.

→ The photo and map show part of the Great Glen in Scotland. Steep, snow-capped mountains rise above the lake on the valley floor.

BLOCK MOUNTAINS

Blocks of rock on either side of a fault may be pushed upwards and downwards, to create a type of mountain called a block mountain. They may, alternatively, slide sideways. In Scotland, a deep trench called the Great Glen has formed along a fault, where rocks have gradually slipped over 100 km sideways. The bottom of the trench has mostly filled with water. This has formed a long string of narrow lakes such as Loch Lochy, shown above.

In many areas, rock movement along faults brings bands of hard and soft rock together. The soft rocks wear away more quickly than the harder rocks. This forms a steep cliff.

Look at the photo and the map

→ Compare the photo and the map. How can you tell from the map that steep slopes edge the lake? (Clue: read 'Using the map'.)

→ How can you tell from the map whether the slopes rise up or drop down to the lake?

→ The landscape in the photo looks completely wild. Can you see signs of human-made changes on the map?

8

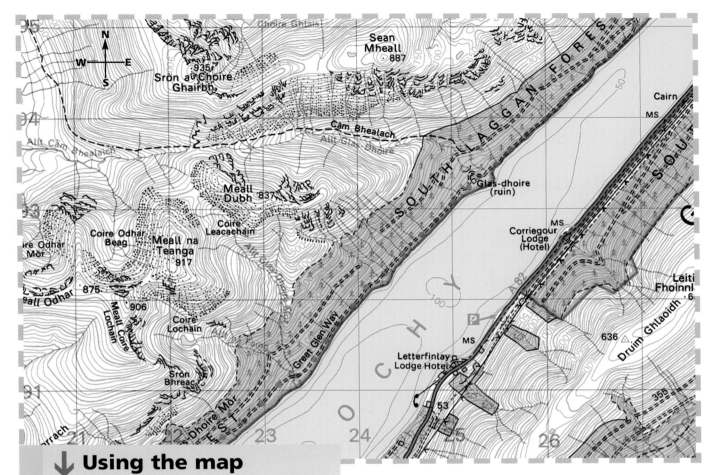

↓ Using the map

Reading contours

In Britain, most maps are made by the central mapping authority, Ordnance Survey (OS). Mapmakers use contour lines to give information about the landscape. Each contour on this map represents 10 m in height. Every fifth line, representing 50 m, is shown darker. Contour lines are also numbered. The numbers always face uphill, so you know which way is up and down.

On the map, find the Letterfinlay Lodge Hotel by the lake. Work out the height of the climb from the hotel to the peak shown to the right.

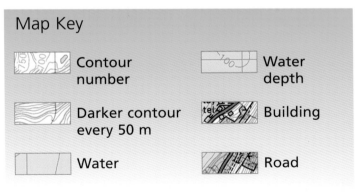

Map Key

Contour number		Water depth	
Darker contour every 50 m		Building	
Water		Road	

TAKING IT FURTHER

• The map on page 4 shows the start of the Great Glen, which runs right across Scotland. Find the line of the Glen on at atlas. It is marked by a string of lakes.

• Look at a local map to see if there are any steep cliffs or hills in your area. Remember the closer the contours, the steeper the slope.

How are mountains shaped?

Millions of years ago, Britain's mountains were much taller than they are today. Over the centuries, they have been worn away by wind, water and ice. This process is called erosion.

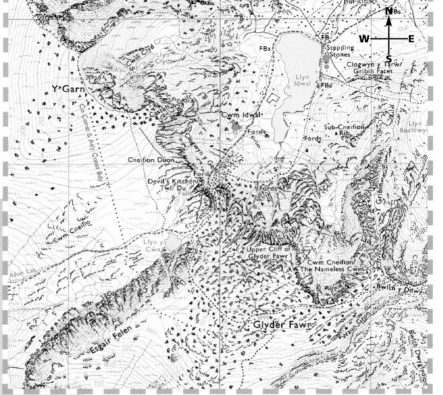

Using the map

Scale on a map
Maps show the landscape shrunk to a particular size, or scale. This large-scale map shows a small area with a lot of detail. Small-scale maps show a bigger area in less detail. The scale of this map is 1:25,000. At this scale every 1 cm on the real map represents 250 m.

Map Key

 Cliff   Path

Scree   Stream

Rock outcrop

0 km   **Scale**   1 km   2 km

0 cm 1 cm 2 cm 3 cm 4 cm 5 cm 6 cm 7 cm 8 cm

EROSION
Erosion happens in several different ways in hills and mountains. As rain, snow and wind beat at the rocks at the surface, small pieces break off. By day, rocks warm up in the sunshine, only to cool again at night. The constant warming and cooling also cracks the rocks. A very extreme form of erosion occurs with glaciation (see pages 14–15)

SPLIT BY ICE

When rain falls, water seeps into cracks in rocks. When water freezes at night, ice splits the rocks open. The rocky pieces tumble downhill, to gather at the foot of mountains in heaps called scree. Small pieces may blow away on the wind. Grit in the wind acts like sandpaper, causing more erosion.

The effects of erosion can be clearly seen in craggy mountains such as Snowdonia in North Wales, shown on the right.

→ **A hiker looks down on the lake shown on the map, Llyn Idwal in North Wales. "Llyn" is the Welsh word for lake.**

Look at the photo and the map

→ **Where do you think the hiker is standing? The shape of the lake provides a clue.**

→ **The photo shows a jumble of scree at the foot of the mountain. Find the same feature on the map.**

→ **The map shows a path leading from Lyn Idwal to Devil's Kitchen at the centre. Contours show the path is steep, but is it up or down?**

→ **Find the straight blue lines running upwards and downwards on the map. The lines form a grid of squares. The grid provides an easy way to guess distance. Each side of the square represents I km.**

→ **Use the blue lines to guess the distance from Llyn Idwal to the smaller lake to the left on the map. Now guess the distance from Devil's Kitchen to where the path meets the lake.**

11

Worn by water

The running water of rivers and streams wears away at hills and mountains. The water comes from rain and snow. The mountains of northern and western Britain are wetter than other areas because they lie in the path of wet winds blowing off the ocean.

RAIN ON THE MOUNTAINS

As moist ocean air meets the mountains, it rises and gets colder. But the cool air can no longer hold its moisture. The moisture condenses to form clouds, which bring rain or snow.

V-SHAPED VALLEYS

Rainwater trickling down steep slopes is channelled into streams. Streams join to make rivers. As rivers and streams flow downhill, they wash stones along with them. As the rocky pieces bounce along the bottom they carve V-shaped valleys.

⬇ Look at the map

Points of a compass
The points of the compass, north, south, east and west, help you find your way. On most maps north is at the top. You can locate a place on a map by giving its direction from somewhere else. For example, the village of Whitchurch lies west of the river loop.

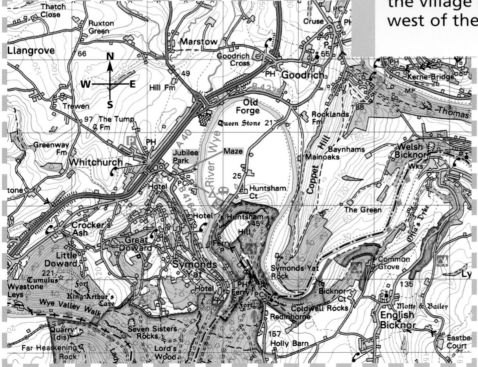

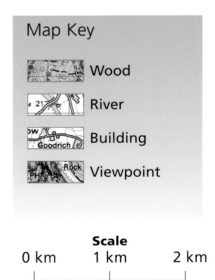

Map Key

	Wood
	River
	Building
	Viewpoint

Scale

0 km	1 km	2 km

| 0 cm | 1 cm | 2 cm | 3 cm | 4 cm |

CURVING RIVERS

Water flowing downhill always takes the easiest route, curving around obstacles such as hills and rocky outcrops. At Symonds Yat Rock in western England, the River Wye has looped north to avoid a rocky ridge at Huntsham Hill.

↑ **This photo shows the view from the high point called Symonds Yat Rock. Find this viewpoint on the map.**

Look at the photo and the map

→ The photo shows the view looking northeast from Symonds Yat Rock. If you look on the map, you will see that a house lies northeast, across the river. Can you see it in the photo?

→ The photo shows a wooded ridge on the right. The bottom edge of the wood curves upwards. Find the same curve on the map.

→ Use a piece of string to trace the river as it loops north from Symonds Yat Rock to Old Forge and then south again. Measure the string using the scale bar and work out the length of the loop.

→ What leisure activity lies northwest of Huntsham Court (at the centre of the loop)? What stone lies north of Huntsham Court?

Sculpted by ice

Some of the most dramatic scenery in Britain's uplands was carved by glaciers. Glaciers are like rivers of ice that flow very slowly downhill, gouging deep valleys as they go.

ICE-AGE BRITAIN

Britain has no glaciers today. But thousands of years ago, the climate was sometimes colder than it is now. During long, cold periods called Ice Ages, most of Britain was covered by a thick sheet of ice.

↓ Using the map

Grid references
On this map the vertical lines showing east to west distances are marked with letters. Horizontal lines showing north to south distances are marked with numbers. You can use the numbers and letters from a grid reference to find places on the map. For example, Loch (Lake) Achtriochtan lies in square B2. The reference gives the bottom left-hand corner of the square.

• What is the grid reference for the house named Achtriochtan, north of the river?

Map Key

░░	Track
░░	Stream
Ⓗ	Viewpoint

Look at the photo and the map

→ **The fast-running River Coe runs along the valley bottom. The river flows in the direction the glacier once flowed.**

→ **The photo shows that the valley is U-shaped as it has a flat bottom and steep sides. How can you tell the valley is U-shaped from the map?**

→ **The map shows many streams joining the river at right-angles. Why do you think this is so?**

GLACIERS

In hills and mountains, masses of ice flowed downwards, forming glaciers. As these giant tongues of ice moved through narrow valleys, they acted like bulldozers, making the valleys wider and deeper. At Glen Coe a deep, U-shaped valley was carved by an Ice-Age glacier.

TAKING IT FURTHER

Find the River Coe on a map of Britain. Where does the river begin and end?

↑ **This photograph shows the deep, U-shaped valley of Glen Coe, in Scotland, which was carved by a glacier.**

Carved by glaciers

As well as deep, U-shaped valleys, glaciers can carve steep peaks and sharp ridges called arêtes.
They can also hollow out circular mountain lakes called corries.
All these features can be seen in Britain's mountains, including Snowdonia in North Wales.

LAYERS OF SNOW

Glaciers are made of packed-down snow. During an Ice Age, snow never melts, but builds up in deep layers. The weight of the snow turns the lower layers to ice. On mountain slopes, glaciers slide downhill.

↓ Using the map

Grid skills

On most maps, both vertical and horizontal lines are numbered. The numbers on this map are taken from the original Ordnance Survey map.

Grid references give east-west distances using the vertical lines first, and then north-south distances using the horizontal lines. Remember this order with the phrase "Along the corridor and up the stairs". For example, Snowdon summit station lies in square 6054.

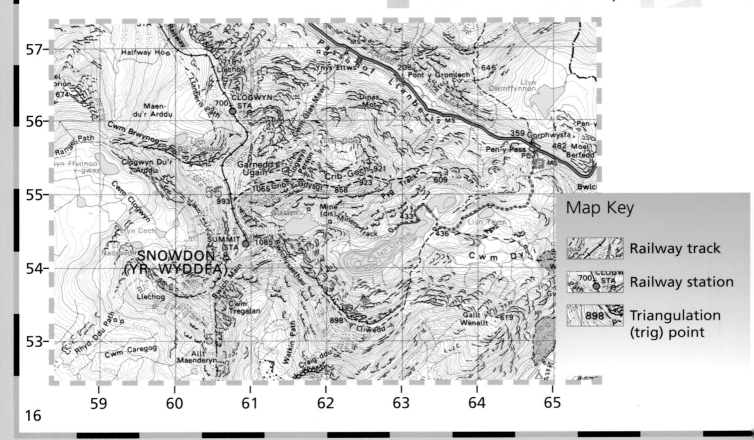

Map Key

Railway track

Railway station

Triangulation (trig) point

↑ **The snowy peak in the photo is Snowdon, the highest mountain in Wales at 1085 m.**

PEAKS, RIDGES AND CORRIES

Where glaciers flow down on all sides of a mountain, they carve a steep, pyramid-shaped peak such as Mount Snowdon in North Wales. Where two glaciers flow side by side, they carve a knife-edge ridge, such as Crib Goch on the flanks of Snowdon. Where ice lingers in hollows, it carves a deep bowl, which fills with water to make a corrie lake. Glaslyn lake below Snowdon is a corrie.

Look at the photo and the map

→ The top of a mountain is marked by a triangulation (trig) point, which shows its height in metres. Find Snowdon's on the map.

→ The photo was taken from the knife-edge ridge of Crib Goch – a scary place to hike! Find it named on the map in 6255.

→ The peak to the right of Snowdon in the photo lies north and slightly east of the mountain. Look on the map to find its name.

→ Describe two features shown in square 6055 – one natural, the other human-made.

→ The Pyg Track, which runs south of Crib Goch, is a famous route up Snowdon. Study the map. What features would you pass climbing Snowdon via the Pyg Track?

Farms and forests

For thousands of years, Britain's hills and mountains have been used for farming. However the style of farming in mountain regions is different to the lowlands.

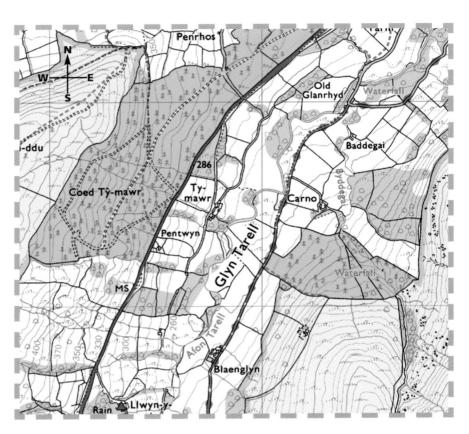

CLIMATE AND SOIL
The climate in mountains and hills is harsher than in lowland areas, with colder, windier, wetter and often snowier conditions. Mountain soil is also thin and stony.

↓ Using the map

Vegetation on maps
Ordnance Survey maps show the types of vegetation growing in the area, such as on this hillside in Wales. Find these features:

 Field boundary

Broad-leaved woodland

Conifer forest

Heath

VEGETATION
The climate and soil affect the type of plants that can grow. For example, broadleaved trees grow in sheltered valleys. Hardy conifer trees grow on hillsides. Mountains and hilltops are too windy for trees, but tough grass or bracken may grow here.

PATTERNS OF FARMING
This map and photo show the typical pattern of farming in Britain's hills and mountains. Crops grow in sheltered fields near the valley bottom. The fertile land here also provides lush pasture for cattle. Conifer trees may be planted on steep hillsides. These trees yield valuable timber. Sheep and sometimes deer graze the bleak heathland along mountain tops.

Look at the photo and the map

→ The photo shows a patchwork of fields in the valley. How are fields shown on the map?

→ Broad-leaved trees (which lose their leaves in autumn) grow on the lower slopes in the photo. What types of trees grow in the area shown on the map?

→ The map shows buildings along the valley bottom. Why do you think farms and houses are located here?

↑ **Cattle and sheep graze in a valley in the Brecon Beacons in South Wales.**

TAKING IT FURTHER
Use a local Ordnance Survey map to find out about the type of farming in uplands near to you.

Find out more about the climate of Britain's mountains on the website: www.met-office.gov.uk. Click the link to mountain weather. Compare mountain climate with the climate where you live.

Mining and energy

Britain's hills and mountains have other uses besides farming. Some areas yield useful minerals. Mountain streams and rivers provide water, and some are used to generate electricity.

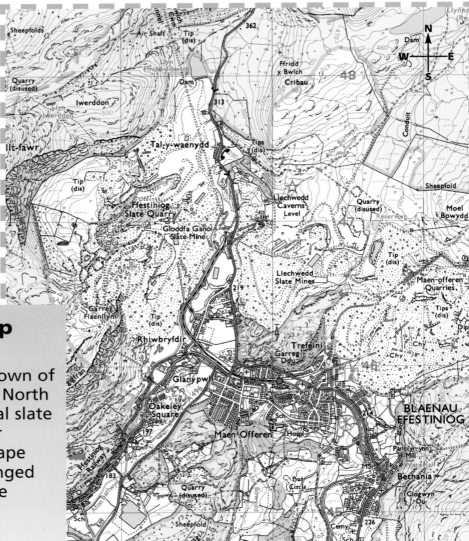

⬇ Using the map

Signs of industry
This map shows the town of Blaenau Ffestiniog in North Wales, where the local slate has been quarried for centuries. This landscape has been greatly changed by industry. Find these features on the map:

 Pit or quarry

 Reservoir

 Railway line

 Tunnel

 Tip

MINING
Mining has gone on in some of Britain's highlands for centuries. In some areas, rocks near the surface yield coal, copper, tin, iron and other minerals. Rocks such as slate and granite are quarried for building. However, mining changes the landscape and can produce pollution. Heaps of waste rock is dumped in mining areas.

↑ This photo shows the landscape around Blaenau Ffestiniog. The railway line was built in the 1860s to transport slate.

Look at the photo and the map

→ Find the railway line on the map. What happens as it passes through the mountains north of the town?

→ The photo shows heaps of waste rock left over from mining. Find this feature on the map.

→ Study the map. List all the ways in which you think industry has affected this landscape.

DAMS AND RESERVOIRS

Upland rivers and streams provide water for towns in the lowlands. The energy of fast-flowing rivers is also used to produce hydroelectric power (HEP). The streams are usually dammed to produce a fast, even flow of water. An artificial lake called a reservoir forms behind the dam. HEP plants don't produce pollution, but reservoirs change the landscape.

TAKING IT FURTHER

Find out about the geology of your local hills or mountains, using the Internet or your local library. For example look at the British Geological website: www.bgs.ac.uk.

Travel in hills

Travel can be difficult in hills and mountains. Rocky peaks, steep slopes and the harsh climate can all create problems for railways and roads.

Roads and railway lines mainly keep to the valleys in hill and mountain country. Mountain ranges are crossed at low points called passes. Mountain roads may be steep, or use sharp curves called hairpin bends to gain height.

Look at the photo and the map

→ The aerial photo does not show the steepness of roads leading out of the valley. How are steep roads shown on the map? (Clue: read 'Using the map'.)

→ The photo shows a road passing over the canal. How is this feature shown on the map?

→ What are the advantages of Todmorden's position? What disadvantages can you think of?

Trains cannot manage steep slopes or sharp bends, but they may use tunnels to pass through the mountains. Bridges are built to carry roads and railway lines across rivers and gorges.

WEATHER PROBLEMS

In winter, snow can close mountain routes, while a coating of ice makes roads slippery and dangerous. Roads are treated with grit or salt so they don't ice over. Bulldozers are used to clear deep drifts of snow.

Upland towns are built where valleys meet, to make travel possible through the mountains. The town, shown on the map and photograph, of Todmorden in the Pennines in northern England, is an example.

TAKING IT FURTHER

Study the network of roads and railways on a map of your nearest mountains. How do local roads and railways cope with obstacles such as hills?

← **An aerial photo of the town of Todmorden, which grew up where valleys allow several routes through the Pennines. Roads, railway lines and a canal all run along the valley bottom. In days gone by, the canal was an important transport link.**

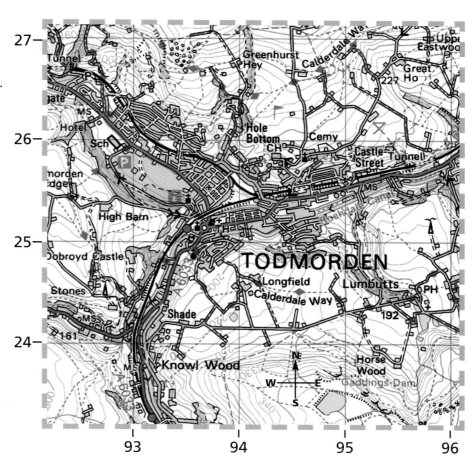

↓ Using the map

Transport symbols

One of the main purposes of most maps is to show the transport network. Major and minor roads, railway lines, stations, bridges, tunnels and car parks are all marked with symbols. Steep roads are shown with arrows. Find these symbols on the map:

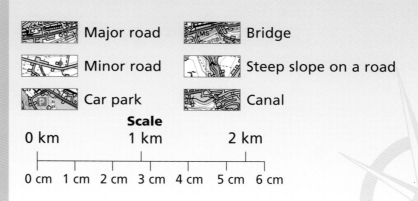

Major road

Bridge

Minor road

Steep slope on a road

Car park

Canal

Scale

0 km   1 km   2 km

0 cm 1 cm 2 cm 3 cm 4 cm 5 cm 6 cm

Towns and villages

Fewer people live in Britain's hills and mountains than in the lowlands. Settlements in the mountains are usually small, partly because of transport difficulties, the harsh climate and steep terrain.

Towns and villages of upland regions are located in the valleys, not on high peaks or windy hilltops. Lower down, the climate is milder, and there is also flat land on which to build. Rivers flowing through valleys provide water for drinking, farming, energy and sometimes for transport.

⬇ Using the map

Ordnance Survey maps like this one have symbols for public buildings such as churches, hospitals, schools and museums. The town hall, library and post office are also marked. Town maps show the names of streets, which can help you to find your way.

Map Key

🏛 **Hall**	Place of worship with tower
	Place of worship with spire, minaret or dome
	Place of worship
Mus	Museum
	Information centre

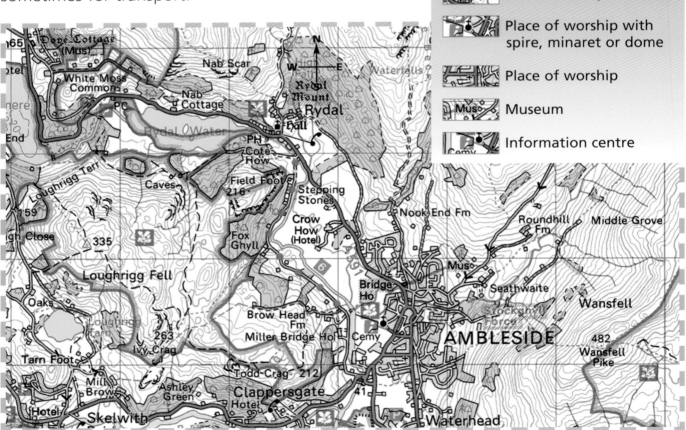

↑ **The photo, and map opposite, show the small town of Ambleside in the heart of the Lake District.**

SUNNY SLOPES

In steep-sided valleys, towns and villages are often located on south-facing slopes that are lit by the Sun even in winter, and are therefore warmer. Snow melts quickly here, so crops grow well. However people are careful not to build under steep cliffs, which could collapse.

Look at the photo and the map

→ **What do you think are the advantages of Ambleside's location? Can you see any disadvantages?**

→ **The photo shows the town's sunny location. Why is this an advantage for the people living there?**

→ **The map shows several churches in Ambleside. Which one appears in the photo?**

TAKING IT FURTHER

• Using a compass together with a map can help to find your way. The red, rotating needle on the compass always points north. Hold the map and turn around until north on the map points in the same direction. Now you know which way to go!

• What is the largest town in the hills or mountains near you? Why do think it grew up in this location?

• Look at the area where you live on a local street map. How are street maps different from Ordnance Survey maps?

25

Tourism and leisure

Mountains and hills are great places to visit. Tourism is one of the main industries in many parts of Britain's uplands.

People go to mountain areas to see the beautiful scenery and enjoy activities such as hiking, climbing, horse-riding, hang-gliding and mountain biking. Aviemore in the Scottish highlands is a winter ski resort. The tourist industry provides work for local people, who run restaurants, activity centres, hotels and shops.

MANAGING TOURISM

Too many visitors can cause problems. Hikers, bikers and horse-riders can erode mountain paths and grassy hillsides. Some tourists drop litter, and their cars bring pollution. Luckily many hills and mountains are part of National Parks or other protected areas. The park authorities look after these wild areas and manage tourism, so that Britain's hills and mountains can be enjoyed for years to come.

↓ Using the map

Leisure maps
Ordnance Survey Explorer maps and tourist maps show activity centres such as ski schools and riding stables. Facilities such as swimming pools, picnic sites and tourist trails are also marked. This allows you to make the most of your visit to the mountains!

• In winter people come to Aviemore for skiing and snowboarding. Study the map, and name five activities that visitors can enjoy at other times of year.
• The photo shows a chair lift that carries skiers up the mountain. How would the lift be useful in summer?

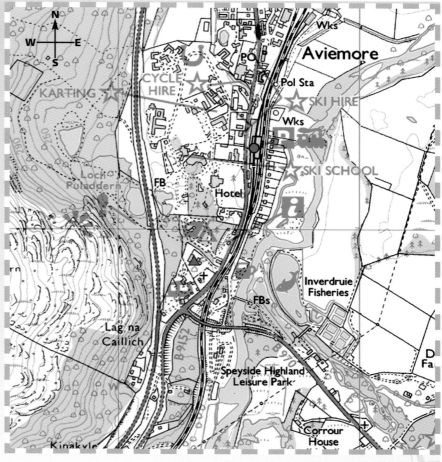

TAKING IT FURTHER

What sports and leisure activities go on in hills or mountains near you? Have you tried any? If so, what is your favourite mountain sport?
• Go to the National Park Authority website, at www.anpa.gov.uk, to see a map of Britain's National Parks. Compare this with the map of Britain's uplands on page 30.
• Write a tourist brochure for Aviemore. Use the map to work out how to attract visitors to the resort.

← **The photo taken near Aviemore shows the reasons for the town's success as a ski resort: thick snow and steep slopes!**

Map Key

	Walk or trail
SKI HIRE	Tourist feature
ℹ	Information centre
	Horse-riding
	Camping and caravan site
Inverd Fishe	Fishing

Check your map skills

These two pages sum up all the map skills that have been introduced in this book. A good understanding of maps will allow you to read the landscape like a book!

MAPS AND SYMBOLS

Maps are drawings of the landscape from above. Maps use symbols, words and colours to show features such as buildings, roads, rivers and forests. The map key explains what the symbols mean. Always check the symbols on the key before you start a walk.

COMPASS POINTS

On most maps north is shown at the top. Compass points, north, south, east, and west, can be used to describe the location of places in relation to somewhere else. You can use a compass to check your direction.

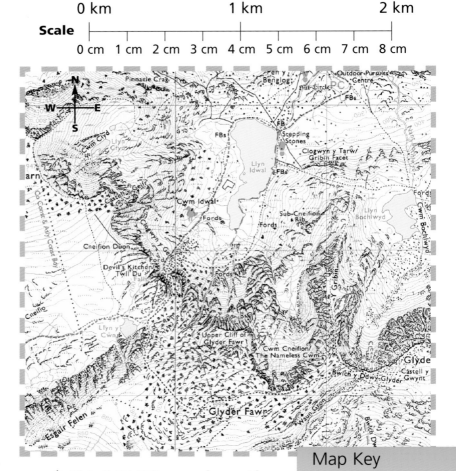

Scale	0 km				1 km			2 km
	0 cm	1 cm	2 cm	3 cm	4 cm	5 cm	6 cm	7 cm	8 cm

↑ This 1:25,000 map shows Llyn Idwal in Snowdonia. At this scale every 1 cm on the real map represents 250 m on the ground.

Map Key

FBs — Footbridge

— Nature reserve

SCALE

Everything on a map is reduced to a particular size, or scale. Large-scale maps, such as 1:25,000, show a small area in a lot of detail. Small-scale maps, such as 1:50,000, show a larger area in less detail.

CONTOUR LINES

Mountains, hills and valleys are shown on maps using contour lines. These lines link places at the same height above sea level. On steep slopes contour lines appear close together. Contour numbers give the height. These numbers always face uphill.

GRIDS AND GRID REFERENCES

A grid of blue lines divide Ordnance Survey maps into squares. Each side of the square represents 1 km. You can use these squares to estimate distance.

The vertical blue lines (running upwards) show east to west distances. The horizontal lines (running sideways) show north to south distances. Grid references plot places on the map. The reference gives the bottom left-hand corner of the square. Grid references give the east to west distance first (the number or letter along the bottom), then the north to south distance (the number or letter along the side).

↓ **This is a 1:50,000 map of the same area. At this scale every 1 cm on the real map represents 500 m on the ground.**

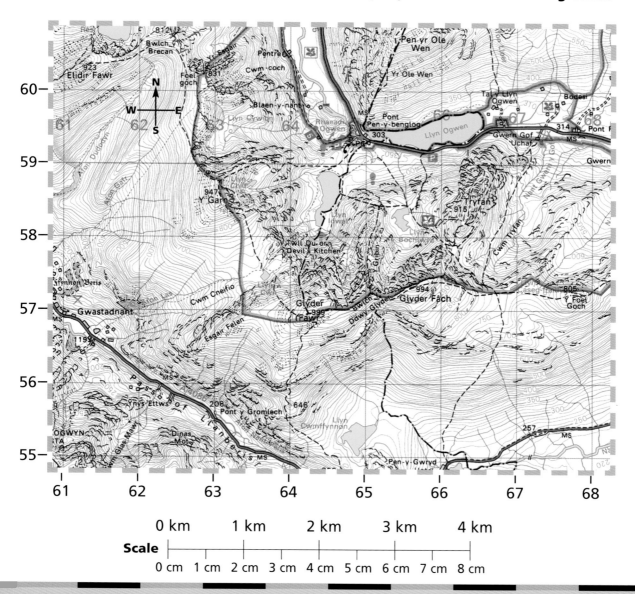

29

Britain's mountains

This map shows the main mountain regions of Britain.

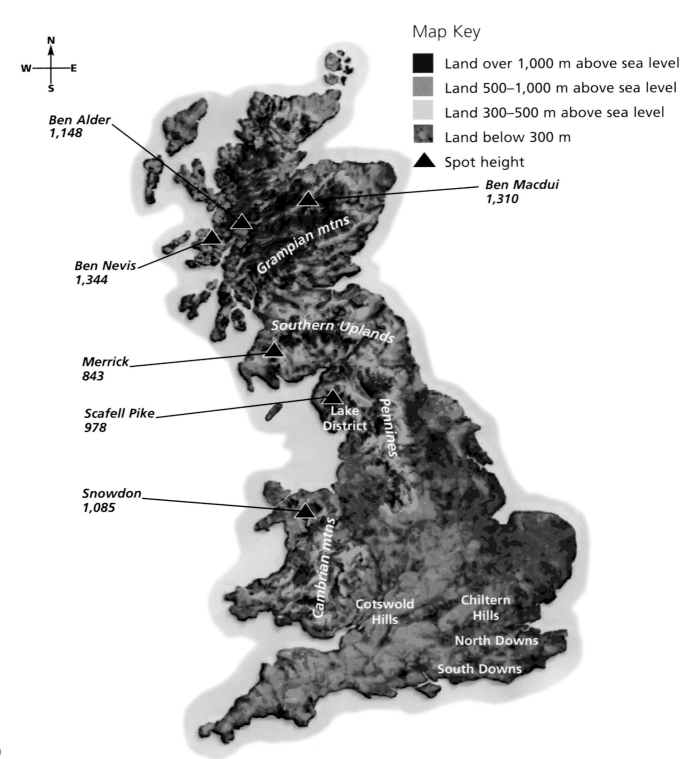

Map Key

- ◼ Land over 1,000 m above sea level
- ▨ Land 500–1,000 m above sea level
- ▦ Land 300–500 m above sea level
- ▨ Land below 300 m
- ▲ Spot height

N W E S

Ben Alder
1,148

Ben Macdui
1,310

Ben Nevis
1,344

Grampian mtns

Southern Uplands

Merrick
843

Scafell Pike
978

Lake District

Pennines

Snowdon
1,085

Cambrian mtns

Cotswold Hills

Chiltern Hills

North Downs

South Downs

Glossary

Aerial view A view of the landscape from above.

Arête A knife-edged ridge carved by two glaciers flowing side by side.

Artificial Not natural, but made by humans.

Block mountain A type of mountain that forms when a block of rock is forced upward between two faultlines.

Broadleaved tree A tree that loses its leaves in winter, such as oak and ash.

Climate The long-term weather pattern in a particular place.

Condense When water changes from a gas into a liquid.

Conifer A tree with narrow waxy leaves, that keeps its leaves all year round.

Contour lines Lines on a map that show the height above sea level.

Corrie A small bowl-shaped hollow in a mountain formed by a glacier. It may contain a lake.

Crust Earth's outer layer.

Erosion When rock or soil is worn away by the weather and carried off by wind, ice or water.

Faultline A deep crack in the rocks of the Earth's crust. Faultlines are often found near the edges of tectonic plates.

Fold mountain A type of mountain that forms where land crumples upward between two colliding tectonic plates.

Geology The study of rocks at the Earth's surface.

Glacier A large mass of ice slowly flowing downhill from high ground.

Gorge A valley walled by cliffs.

Horizontal Lying flat. Horizontal lines run across the page.

Hydroelectric power Electricity that is generated using fast-flowing water.

Ice Age A long, cold period in the past, during which ice covered much more of Earth's surface than it does today.

Location A place or the position of something.

Minerals The non-living substances from which rocks are made.

Mountain An area of high ground more than 500 m above sea level.

Ordnance Survey Britain's official map-making organisation.

Outcrop An area of rock at the Earth's surface.

Pass A low point in the mountains where a road or path crosses the range.

Range The name given to a group of mountains.

Reservoir An artificial lake created by a dam and used to store water.

Rotate To turn in a circle.

Scree Heaps of rock found on the side and at the foot of mountains, and worn from the crags above.

Spot height A point on a map that gives the height above sea level.

Summit The top of a mountain or hill.

Symbol A sign, or something that represents something else.

Tectonic plate One of the giant rocky slabs that make up the Earth's outer layer.

Upland Land that is more than 300 m above sea level.

Vegetation The plants that grow in a particular area.

Vertical Upright. Vertical lines run up and down.

Index

FURTHER INFORMATION WEBSITES:

Websites on mountains:
www.mountains2002.org/
www.mountainpartnership.org

Websites on maps:
Ordnance Survey: www.ordnancesurvey.co.uk/mapzone
www.multimap.co.uk
Type in place names or postcodes to see aerial views and maps of places in Britain.

Weather and climate:
The Met Office: www.met-office.gov.uk

Conservation organisations:
National Parks Authorities: www.anpa.gov.uk
The National Trust: www.nationaltrust.org.uk/
Environment Agency: www.environment-agency.gov.uk

The BBC's geography and natural history website:
www.bbc.co.uk/sn

These are the lists of contents for each title in
Mapping Britain's Landscapes:

Cities, Towns and Villages
What are cities, towns and villages? • Where do settlements grow up? • Settlements by rivers • Settlements by the sea • Mining and industry • Village life • Urban life • How do settlements grow and change? • Britain's capital • New developments • Getting about • Looking to the future • Check your map skills • Britain's towns and cities

Coasts
Mapping coasts • Wearing away coasts • Cliffs • Beaches and dunes • Changing shape • Where rivers meet coasts • Coastal settlements • Ports and harbours • Tourism and leisure • Islands • Changing sea levels • Coastal management • Check your map skills • Britain's coastline

Hills and Mountains
What are hills and mountains? • How do hills and mountains form? • Cliffs and block mountains • How are mountains shaped? • Worn by water • Sculpted by ice • Carved by glaciers • Farms and forests • Mining and energy Travel in hills • Towns and villages • Tourism and leisure • Check your map skills • Britain's mountains

Rivers
Mapping rivers • Rivers and the water cycle • How do rivers change the land? • Rivers in the highlands • Rivers in the lowlands • Where rivers meet the sea • When rivers flood • River settlements • Transport and crossing places • Water and work • Dams and reservoirs • Rivers and recreation Check your map skills • Britain's rivers